Mom's Homemade

A Humorous Look at Family Stress

by Kimberly Chambers

Copyright © 1999 Great Quotations, Inc.

All rights reserved. Written permission must be secured from the publisher to use or reproduce any part of this book, except for brief quotations in critical reviews or articles.

Cover Illustration by Design Dynamics

Published by Great Quotations Publishing Company
Glendale Heights, IL

Library of Congress Catalog number: 99-072986
ISBN: 1-56245-383-1

Printed In Hong Kong

This book is dedicated to my terrific family and wonderful friends.

If at first you can't find something,
try looking under the couch cushion.

Grandma is upset that you let the children play with a mouse--never mind that it's on the computer.

Stress is: Hearing the repairman say, "I've never seen anything like this before."

You're the only one in the house who knows how to change the toilet paper roll.

Don't worry! Your husband will notice
your new hairstyle--about a month
after you have it done.

It's hard to say who has more toys--
your children or your spouse.

The good news: Your child started kindergarten. The bad news: You're still wearing maternity clothes.

Don't ATM machines know that they're supposed to give you extra spending money?

They can't remember to shut the refrigerator door, but they remember everything you said about Aunt Jane.

Household Rule: Your purse is
considered community property.

When teaching your family table manners, be sure to include your spouse.

When you take your first sip of morning coffee, you realize it was yesterday's.

Your mother-in-law offers to stay for a week to help you "get your house in order."

You have more money invested in your child's dental work than in the stock market.

Stress is: Remembering your spouse's
birthday-- the day after.

When you receive flowers from your spouse, you wonder what he's up to!

If you have a teenager and the phone rings, don't worry--it's not for you.

Stress is: Hearing your dry cleaner say, "What clothes?" when you come to pick them up.

Your relatives surprise you with a impromptu weekend visit on the night of your wedding anniversary.

You know it's dinner time when the telephone solicitors start calling.

Your child wants to know if he can eat the fish stick he's been saving under the couch.

Life would be easier if we could
choose our family members.

Stress is: Setting your alarm for p.m.
instead of a.m.

Household Rule: Always double the contractor's bid and triple the time required to complete the job.

Grandpa's neatest trick is taking out his false teeth.

You tried to interview a maid--she ran out of your house screaming.

Stress is: Getting a ticket with
carpool children in the back seat.

Your towels disappear every time
Uncle Buck stays for the weekend.

Funny how "It's probably none of my business", is always followed by the word "but."

Stress is: Getting home at midnight
to discover your kids locked the
baby-sitter outside.

You're not sure if a "Wildlife Refuge" sign would best describe your kids or the number of stray pets you have.

You have to hire an accountant to balance your family budget.

Stress is: Sitting in a traffic jam on the way to the delivery room.

Your frequent flyer miles expire the day before you try to book a family vacation.

On April 16, your spouse wants to know if he was supposed to do the taxes.

Need an expert in crisis management?
Hire a mom!

Your spouse asks what **you** did with
the things he can't find.

Your dust bunnies certainly multiply
like rabbits.

Stress is: Watching a shopping cart roll into your car from across the parking lot.

When it's time to change clothes,
your child transforms into an octopus.

Are the straps on the grocery cart to keep your child from grabbing things?

Household Rule: Leave a little bit in
the container, then you won't have to
throw it away.

Your spouse gives you an exercise
video for your birthday.

48

Your child tells the cashier that she's really six after hearing that children under five eat free.

Stress is: Waiting in the express lane behind someone with a full cart of groceries.

It's a bad sign when your husband
faints during childbirth class.

When you're really mad, hide the batteries to the remote control.

Your children have to show you how to use the computer.

53

Your husband may fix things for a living, but he can't fix anything around the house.

Can you deduct a late fee from the doctor's bill when he makes you wait?

You only hear that the apple doesn't fall too far from the tree when your kids get into trouble.

Your children list pizza, hamburgers, hot dogs, and ice cream as the four major food groups.

It's great seeing your relatives. You get to hear the same old stories over and over and over...

You catch your child imitating rude gestures he learned from a discourteous driver.

The most difficult obstacle course in the world: walking through your house in the dark.

Stress is: Realizing <u>all</u> of your child's friends are imaginary.

Your child wants to know where the
money tree grows.

Household Rule: Before the relatives visit, hang a sign reading,"Unsolicited Advice Prohibited."

Your kids spend most of their time in "time-out."

Your in-laws brag that your child takes after you (but only when your child acts up).

Household Rule: Teach your family
how to screen your telephone calls.

Stress is: Realizing you sound exactly
like your parents.

Ask your teenager (they know it all anyway)!

Motto of the Perfect Relative: "If you want my opinion, you'll have to ask."

It's hard to say what's more spoiled--
sour milk or your children after
they've spent a week with their
grandparents!

Your car is in the repair shop the week you're supposed to drive for the carpool.

No, honey, petroleum jelly is not a good conditioner for your hair.

At your house, sibling rivalry is more like sibling warfare.

Your children seem to think you own
the electric company.

Stress is: Hearing a loud crash in the crystal department followed by an "Oops!" from your child.

You know your relatives were listening
to your phone conversations when
they ask you questions about it later.

Stress is: Being scheduled for jury duty the week of your family vacation.

Road Trip Tip: If all else fails, threaten to stop the car.

Can you send your relatives to time-out?

79

Food for thought: Is it mold or a
science fair project?

Your son tells grandma how much he likes her legs, because his favorite color is blue.

Your children keep a list of grievances to discuss in front of your relatives.

When you least expect it, your child will transform into the ultimate human tape recorder.

Stress is: Noticing the "Lane Closed" sign after you've waited in line for an eternity.

When the goin' gets tough, send them
to Grandma's!

Your sister "couldn't help but overhear" your private discussion.

Your child wants to know if his school
is for sale because it's having an
open house

Stress is: Noticing that none of the ants are in the ant farm.

Thankfully, Grandma got her own
1-800 number.

Your junk drawer has taken over an
entire room.

The grocery store takes automatic
deductions from each paycheck.

If your spouse takes your car, he'll leave you his car without any gas.

In your family, you're known as an out-law instead of an in-law.

Stress is: Returning from the grocery store without the one thing you went to buy.

Your mother-in-law's sentences begin,
"If it were me...".

Stress is: The annual battle over who goes to which house for the holidays.

You install a lock on your medicine cabinet before your relatives come over.

You have more phone lines than household members.

Household Rule: Children will wait
until you're in public before asking
the most embarrassing questions.

The dog house has two rooms--one for Fido, the other for your husband.

Your nights on the town have been
replaced with video rentals and frozen
dinners.

Your teenager finally got his driver's
license--and it only took 5 tries!

Stress is: Realizing you had the winning combination after the contest expired.

Things that don't mix: children, pets, and white carpeting.

You wish you'd paid more attention in class now that you have to help your kids with their homework.

Stress is: Finding out about your child's project the night before it's due.

If you had to transport any more children, you'd need a commercial license.

You hide your children's videos so you
don't have to watch them again.

Your house is so dirty, even the bugs
are complaining.

Stress is: Thinking of a different meal for dinner every night.

Household Rule: If your kids can't find something, it will take you three minutes. If your husband can't find something, it will take you three seconds.

Does a family vacation mean you have
to take the kids?

Stress is: Getting a speeding ticket in
your child's school zone.

Your favorite time of year is "Back to School"!

114

Are <u>all</u> of the baby-sitters busy, or is it that they don't want to keep your kids?

Why does your spouse have golf clubs in the backseat when he said he was going to the office?

Everyday should be Mother's Day
Out!

For some reason, your child's report card is covered with correction fluid.

Stress is: Setting off the house
alarm at 2:00 a.m. with a house full of
overnight guests.

Maybe you should get a job so you could at least get a day off!

Junior wants to know why Daddy is making the goldfish swim in the toilet.

Your last baby-sitter quit due to
mental anguish.

Stress is: Finding out your son is
dating your boss's daughter.

The last day of school = your last day of sanity.

You find it difficult to talk to an adult
without using "kiddie" language.

Stress is: Discovering your child's
library book is overdue from last year.

Your kids organized a labor strike
against household chores.

Stress is: Realizing you forgot to give
your child lunch money.

Consider it an accomplishment if half
of your errands get done.

It was an unlisted phone number--until
your teenager gave it out to everyone.

Your children have names for every
inanimate object in the house.

Household Rule: Child safety locks =
broken finger nails.

Stress is: The only passing grade on your child's report card is in gym class.

The one time you miss a meeting,
you're elected committee chair.

Grandpa doesn't want the kids playing on the computer because they might catch a computer virus.

Stress is: Running into your boss at the mall after you've called in sick.

You even take care of your kids
electronic pets!

Eavesdropping, overhearing, what's the difference?

When you tell your spouse you want to add a little spice to your life, he gives you some salt.

A child's creed: If I leave the mess long enough, Mom will clean it up.

Stress is: Your child bought a self-help book on dealing with difficult parents.

Your child used permanent markers to "color" her hair.

142

You fantasize that the junk in your attic consists of priceless antiques.

Household Rule: If you're running late, no one else will be in a hurry.

Stress is: Finding out your entire tax refund was spent on a big screen TV.

Your kids don't understand why you spend so much time in the kitchen.

No, honey, you only put peanut butter
in your hair to get the gum out!

Stress is: Discovering your child trades his nutritious lunch for soft drinks and candy bars.

Sure I'll take care of your problem-- right after my manicure and herbal massage.

Your company announced cut backs
after you'd already spent your bonus.

Household Rule:
Always verify when your kids say, "But Dad said it was okay."

You leave out trash to see how well the maid really cleans.

Your spouse doesn't understand why you clean the house before the maid comes.

You have to pick out clothes for your spouse as well as your children.

"No, Aunt Edna, Mommy won't be able to go to your house next week. She's planning on having a migraine."

You nominate yourself for Parent of the Year.

You know you're working too much
when you spend more time with your
office mates than with your own
family.

Stress is: Your mother-in-law buys a
new house--two houses down from
yours.

Household Rule: No one wants to help
cook dinner, but everyone wants to
help eat it.

Your child knows more state capitol's
than you do.

160

Stress is: Realizing the club meeting
is at your house when you see all of
the cars parked in front.

Household Rule: If you can read the
name on the message, you won't be
able to read the phone number.

Everyone assumes when they're not
busy, you're not busy either.

Stress is: Hearing the cashier yell, "Price Check!" when you're buying personal items.